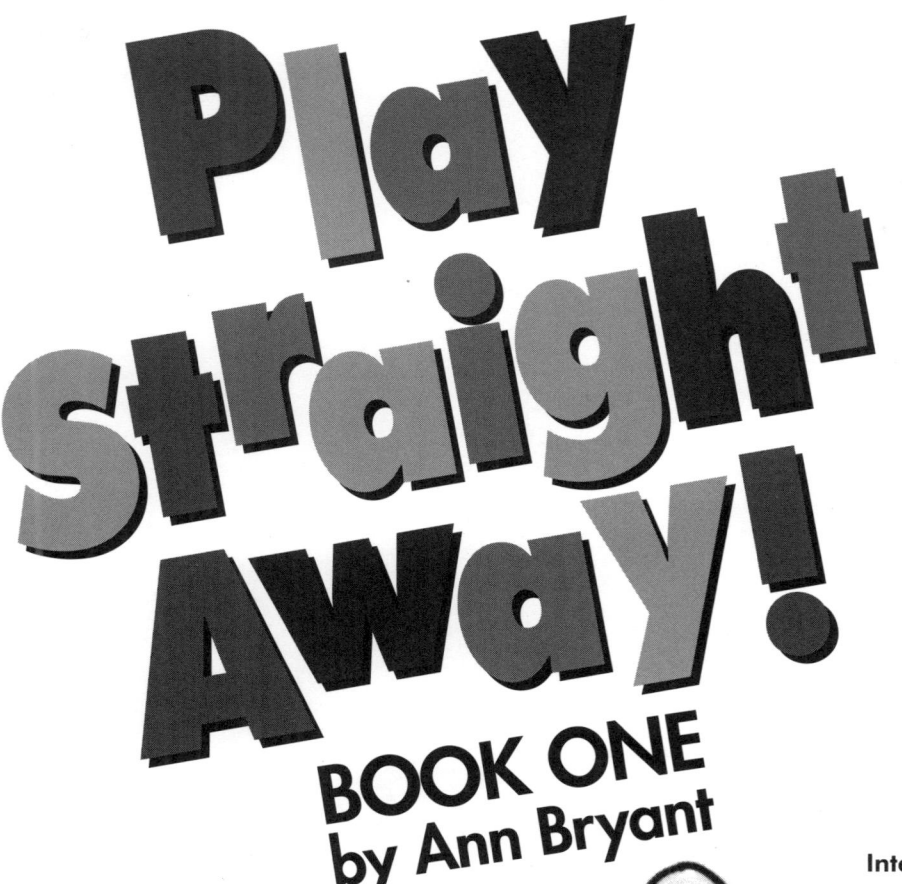

Play Straight Away!
BOOK ONE
by Ann Bryant

Series Editor
Sadie Cook

Illustrations by
Paul Selvey, John Good Holbrook Ltd

Cover design by
John Good Holbrook Ltd

Music Setting by
Barnes Music Engraving Ltd

Published 1999

EXCLUSIVE DISTRIBUTORS

International Music Publications Limited
Griffin House, 161 Hammersmith Road
London W6 8BS, England

International Music Publications Limited
20 Rue de la Ville-L'Eveque, 75008 Paris, France

International Music Publications GmbH, Germany
Marstallstraße 8, D-80539 München, Germany

Nuova Carisch S.p.A.
Via Campania, 12
20098 San Giuliano Milanese - Milano, Italy

Danmusik
Vognmagergade 7, DK-1120 Copenhagen K, Denmark

Warner/Chappell Music Australia Pty Ltd
3 Talavera Road, North Ryde, New South Wales 2113, Australia

Warner Bros. Publications Ins Inc
16800 NW 48th Avenue, Miami Fl 33014, USA

© International Music Publications Limited
Griffin House 161 Hammersmith Road London W6 8BS England

Reproducing this music and any other part of this publication in any form is illegal and forbidden by the Copyright, Designs and Patents Act 1988

Caring for the Environment
This book has been produced with special regard to the environment. We have insisted on the use of acid-free, neutral-sized paper made from pulps which have not been elemental bleached and have sought assurance that the pulp is farmed from sustainable forests.

Dear Teacher / Parent / Helper,

Welcome to Dodgem land, where the PLAY STRAIGHT AWAY BOOKS take place!

ABOUT THIS BOOK

This recorder book is for young beginners. There are no music notes to read, only letters. Each letter requires certain holes to be covered on the recorder. In the pictures of the recorder throughout the book, the black dots show which holes to cover. Children can learn with the greatest possible ease from PLAY STRAIGHT AWAY because every piece uses the rhythm (and sometimes the tune) of a well known song such as 'The Grand Old Duke Of York'. This means that **you don't need to have any understanding of music notation. Just follow the letters**.

By the end of this first book, children will have acquired the following abilities:
- To recognise the letters D, C, B, A, G, F♯, E, D.
- To understand that each letter requires a different combination of fingers covering the holes.
- To cover the holes properly.
- To follow the music on the page without a guiding finger to help.
- To do all this within a rhythmic framework.
- To make a nice sound while playing.

Imagine how demanding all this would be if the child was also having to cope with reading properly notated music. This is why I save that for book 2. Both books are full of fun and Dodgem Land magic because the story of Cute King Dodge and Nobby Gnome runs throughout each book.

HOW TO USE THIS BOOK

Learn each new piece together, then ask the child/children to practise it. Make sure they understand what is meant by practising. They are trying to make the piece sound better.

This may involve:
1) Making sure the holes really are covered properly. (A good way of checking is to press a finger firmly over a hole and then look at that finger pad. Is there an imprint of a complete circle?)
2) Making sure the piece flows along without gaps or hesitations. Is the child sure which holes must be covered for all the different letters in that piece? Are they moving from one note to the next quickly enough? Only repetition achieves this, and that is an important lesson in itself.
3) Making sure the rhythm sounds like the rhythm of the given tune title.
4) Making sure they aren't blowing too hard? (See first session overleaf.)

Always give lots of praise and try to have regular little concerts to differentiate between practice and the final performance. Give stars or stickers for each piece played to the best of the child's ability. At first this may mean giving a star for something extremely hard on the ear, but if this is the best the child can do at this stage, then that's fine. It doesn't matter that the child's playing will probably be very slow, particularly in the earlier pieces, as long as the rhythm of the piece is maintained. If the child is really struggling after quite a few pieces, either give a philosophical shrug and try again in a few months time, or slow down the pace.

PACE-SLOWERS

Here's a few examples of how to slow down the pace and give the child/children a chance to revise what they have already learnt:
1) Play over old pieces.
2) Spend some time following the music by pointing to each letter and saying that letter (in the right rhythm for the piece). Alternatively, the child/children could say the letters while you play the piece.
3) Sing the piece through together.
4) Play a game of 'Copy Me'. For this game, YOU play a note and the child/children copy by WATCHING. At school you could dot around the class, saying a child's name then playing a note yourself, which that child must imitate. Keep changing the notes. Extend this game by playing two then three notes to be copied. The three notes could be, for example, A B A or B B C. A variation of that game is to say the letter or letters (up to three) of the notes that the child should then play. The variation here is that the child must know their notes, rather than copying what they see YOU doing. You could turn this into a team game by awarding points for correct note playing.
5) Play one of the pieces yourself. Can the child/children say which piece it is?
6) Play one of the pieces with a deliberate mistake. Can they identify the mistake? Again this could be adapted in the classroom as a team game.
7) Have the front row of children playing the first line of music to one of the pieces, the second row the second line, and so on. This means that the children have to follow the music to know when it's their turn to play – so don't always start with the front row.

These 'pace slowers' also provide general consolidation and break the intensity of continual playing.

In the classroom situation, try to have all of the children involved as much of the time as possible. If they are not actually playing they could be following the music with a finger, or they could be pretending to play by covering the correct holes but making no sound. Sometimes the children should simply listen to each other. Ask them at the end: Did it sound nice? Was it too loud? Too squeaky? Too slow? Does it deserve a star? I tend to use the following degrees of reward, all in gold pen: 1) small tick 2) big tick 3) small star 4) big star. If a child judges correctly, from listening carefully, what I'm going to award another child for their performance, I give that child a star (in ordinary pen) on their hand. This makes the valuable exercise of listening and appraising, much more fun.

In addition to stars and ticks, there are also stickers included at the back of the book. When the child/children have completed a piece if there is space for a sticker use it as a reward – can they find the right sticker to stick? (They're displayed in order at the back.)

Now you are ready for the very first session. Good luck and have fun!

THE FIRST SESSION

The picture on page 5 shows the best way to hold the recorder until page 18. This may look unprofessional, but young children's hands are too small to cope with the correct position straight away, and trying to do so is frustrating when there are so many other things to think about. Get into the following routine for holding the recorder this way:

1) The helper (teacher or parent) sits facing the child, who sits cross legged on the floor. Have something beginning with B, eg a box, on your left, (child's right). Remember that the helper and the child are mirroring each other all the time.
2) The child grasps the recorder in their left hand with the holes facing the helper. (S)he sticks out the right hand to the right side, pointing to the box and saying, 'b' for box and 'b' for bottom. (S)he then grasps the recorder at the bottom with the right hand.
3) The child sticks out the left hand to the left side, and does a repeated 'pincers' action with the thumb and index finger of this left hand while bringing the hand closer and closer to the top hole of the recorder, saying 'pinch' all the while, and finally closing the 'pincers' so the index finger covers the top hole at the front and the thumb covers the hole at the back. At this point they say 'Got you!'

Repeat this routine several times and also use it at the start of the next few sessions until it comes quickly and easily. Always mirror the child. You do the routine too. The sound made when the recorder is blown with these two holes covered, is called B. All the sounds have letter names, and in music we call the sounds notes.

Make sure the child is not bowed over with the bottom of the recorder touching their leg. They should be able to look down the holes comfortably.

Each time a sound is made, the tongue should make the same movement as for saying the sound 't' slowly. Keep reminding the child about this. It rarely comes naturally. Children often blow, as though blowing out a candle. Look out for this and try to correct it whenever it happens.

Now you are ready for the first piece.

5

Follow Me To Dodgem Land!

(rhythm: first part of *This Old Man*)

B

B B B
Dod - gem Land.

B B B
Dod - gem Land.

B B B B B B B
Fol - low me to Dod - gem Land.

It's great in Dodgem Land. You can go whizzing around everywhere in very fast jeeps. And you never bump into anyone because you simply press a certain button, and the jeep will go up in the air!

insert sticker

L.H.

Let's Go Racing

(rhythm: first part of *Frère Jacques*)

A A A A A A A A
Let's go rac - ing, hel - ter skel - ter,

A A A   A A A
in my car,   in my car!

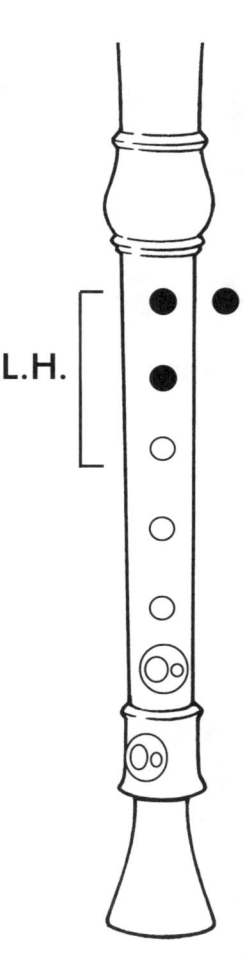

Racing Through The Sky

(rhythm: first part of *Sing A Song Of Sixpence*)

B	B	B	B	A	A	B	B	B	B	A
Rac-	ing	through	the	sky	as	hap-	py	as	can	be,

B	B	B	B	A	A	B	B	B	B	A
Watch	the	clouds	go	by	and	see	who	you	can	see!

The only people you can't see are the cave people. Nobody knows much about the cave people because they keep themselves to themselves.

insert sticker

Nobby Gnome

(rhythm: *Polly Put The Kettle On*)

C

B	**B**	**A**	**A**	**B**	**B**	**C**	
Nob	- by	Gnome	is	quite	a	star,	
B	**B**	**A**	**A**	**B**	**B**	**C**	
Peo	- ple	come	from	near	and	far,	
B	**B**	**A**	**A**	**B**	**B**	**C**	**C**
Just	to	hear	him	"la	la	la",	he
B		**B**		**C**			
ne	-	ver		stops . . .			

… except if anybody comes too close. But wait a minute … I think I can hear someone coming! Stand up! Quick! It's the King!

Cute King Dodge Of Dodgem Land

(rhythm: *Twinkle, Twinkle, Little Star*)

C	C	C	C	B	B	B	A	A	A	A	B	B	B
Here's	the	King	of	Dod-	gem	Land,	Cute	King	Dodge	is	ve	- ry	grand.

C	C	C	C	B	B	B	A	A	A	A	B	B	B
If	you	see	him	you	must	stand,	sit -	ting	down's	com -	plete	- ly	banned.

C	C	C	C	B	B	B	C	C	B	B	C	C	C
Here's	the	King	of	Dod-	gem	Land,	Cute	King	Dodge	is	ve	- ry	grand.

The trouble is, everyone always feels like laughing when they see King Dodge because he doesn't wear a crown, he wears a big chef's hat! It's such a funny sight that there are always crowds of people outside the palace gates, waiting to catch a glimpse of him.

insert sticker

People Wait Outside The Gate

(rhythm: *1, 2, 3, 4, 5, Once I Caught A Fish Alive*)

D

C   **C**   **D**   **D**   **C**
Peo - ple   al - ways   wait

A   **A**   **A**   **A**   **B**   **B**   **C**
Right out - side the pal - ace gate,

C   **C**   **D**   **D**   **C**
Just   in   case they spy

A   **A**   **B**   **B**   **C**   **C**   **C**
Dodge the King go driv - ing by.

One day the people at the gate got a shock because Cute King Dodge came out of the palace wearing a very stern look on his face underneath his chef's hat, and climbed into a huge, open-topped jeep.

insert sticker

L.H.

12

The King's Looking Cross

(rhythm: *The Wheels On The Bus*)

B **A** **A A C** **C** **A** **A** **C**
The King's look-ing cross, so ve - ry cross,

B **B** **D** **B** **B** **D**
ve - ry cross, ve - ry cross,

B **A** **A A C** **C** **A** **A** **C**
The King's look-ing cross, so ve - ry cross,

D **D** **C**
Let's guess why.

Off went the jeep heading out of town towards the caves. The reason the King was looking so cross was because one of his servants had told him that the cave people didn't like him. But this wasn't true.

insert sticker

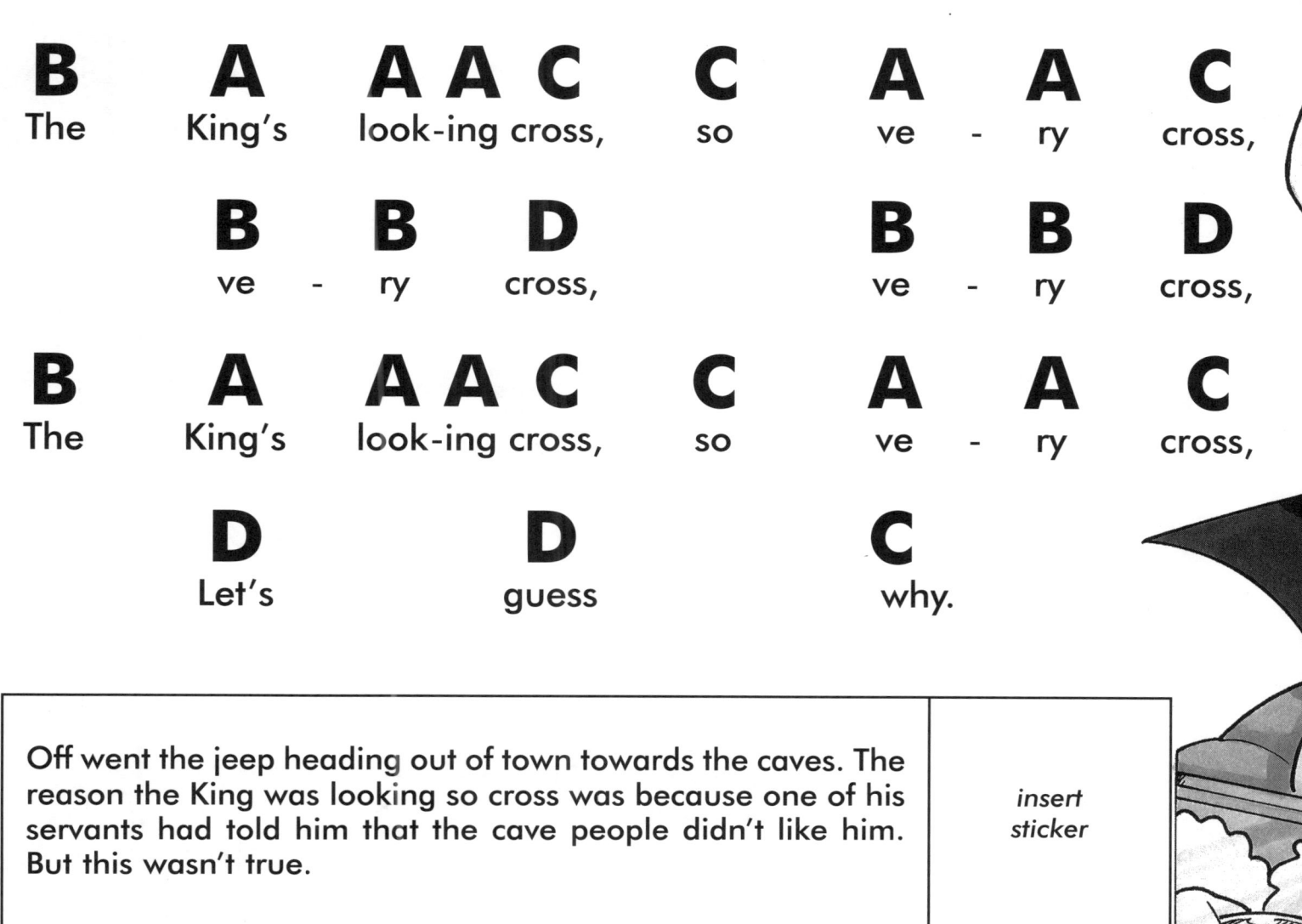

Yuk!

(rhythm: *London Bridge Is Falling Down*)

B	B	B	B	C	C	B
"How	re -	volt -	ing,"	said	the	King.

A	A	D		A	A	D
"Nas -	ty	caves,"		said	the	King.

B	B	B	B	C	C	B
"Hor -	rid	peo -	ple!"	said	the	King.

D		B		C	C	
"Yuk!		I'm		go -	ing!"	

The cave people felt hurt that the King thought they were horrid, and that the caves where they lived were nasty and revolting. They thought the King might like them better if he saw some of their carvings. "Let's show him the beautiful carving of the King, himself," said Deidre. And the other cave people thought that was a great idea.

insert sticker

This One's Of You, Your Majesty

(rhythm: *Here We Go Round The Mulberry Bush*)

B	B	B	B	B	B	B	B
Look	o -	ver	here,	your	ma	- jes	- ty,

A	A	A	A	A	A	A	A
Your	ma -	jes	- ty,	your	ma	- jes	- ty.

G	G	G	G	G	G	G	G
This	one's	of	you,	your	ma	- jes	- ty,

G	G	A	A	A	A	G	G
And	we	real	- ly	hope	you	like	it.

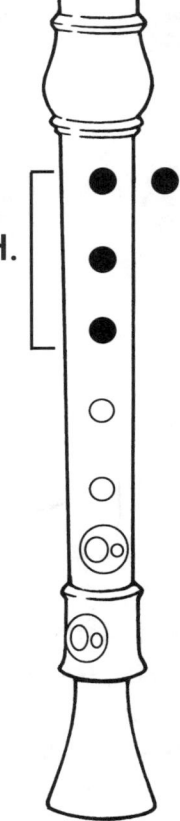

But the King did NOT like it. "Why have you made me look such a fool in that hat?" he demanded, going red in the face and scowling horribly. The cave people were very upset. "We tried to make the carving look just like you, your majesty," said Dave in a gentle voice. And that made the King go beserk!

insert sticker

How Can You Say Such A Thing?

(rhythm: *Hickory Dickory Dock*)

B	B	B	C	C	C	D
How	can	you	say	such	a	thing?

B	B	B	B	C	C	C	D
I	look	like	a	chef,	not	a	King!

G	G		G	G		G	A	A	G
You're	hor	-	rid	peo	-	ple,	like	I	thought.

B	B	B	A	A	A	G
How	can	you	say	such	a	thing?

And with that, the King stomped out of the caves. As he rode off in his jeep he called out "And don't think I'm ever coming here again!" It's a good job that Cute King Dodge didn't hear the song on the next page, or goodness knows what he would have done!

insert sticker

16

The Cute Old King Called Dodge

(tune: *The Grand Old Duke Of York*)

B **A** **G** **G** **G** **G** **G**
Oh the Cute Old King called Dodge,

G **A** **A** **A** **A** **A**
He makes you want to stare,

A **B** **B** **B** **B** **C** **C** **C**
'Cos fan - cy that, his crown's a hat,

C **C** **B** **B** **A** **A** **G**
And he does - n't seem to care.

But the cave people would never dream of singing any nasty songs like that. They were too kind. When the King had roared off in his jeep, they all began to cry.	*insert sticker*

17

Poor Cave People

(rhythm: *Yellow Submarine*)

D	C	B	A	A G	G G	G G
Poor	cave	peo	- ple,	they all	be-gan	to weep,

A	A A	A A		G	G G	G G
All	be-gan	to weep,		all	be-gan	to weep.

D	C	B	A	A G	G G	G G
Cute	King	Dodge	kept	on shout - ing in		his jeep,

A	A A	A A		G	G G	G G
Shout - ing in		his jeep,		shout - ing in		his jeep.

And high on the hill-top sat Nobby Gnome, frowning and thinking. He had heard every word that had been said, and he felt very angry that the King had upset the poor cave people.

insert sticker

Nobby Gnome's Magic Spell

(rhythm: *Happy Birthday To You*)

G	G	G	G	B	D
I	am	wav-	ing	my	wand.

G	G	G	G	B	D
Iz-	zy	woo	iz-	zy	wiz

G	G	G	G	B	D	D
Turn	the	peo-	ple	to	stone	but

D	D	D	D	D	G
Leave	the	King	as	he	is!

And as Nobby stood high on his hill-top waving his wand and chanting the words of this magic spell, something incredible happened in Dodgem Land. Every single person except for the cave people and the King turned to stone!

insert sticker

Statues Of Stone

(rhythm: *Three Blind Mice*)

G   **G**   **G**   **A**   **A**   **A**
What   a   sight!   What   a   sight!

B   **B**   **B**   **B**   **C**   **C**   **C**   **C**
Stat - ues of stone,   stat - ues of stone.

C D D D D D D D D C C C C C C C C
The mum-mies, dad-dies and child-ren too, the gran-nies and gran-dads and bab-ies too,

C B B B B B B B B B B A A G
The pal-ace, the sold-iers, the ser-vants and all, but not the King!

So King Dodge found himself all alone in a land full of statues. He was furious!	*insert sticker*

20

Nobby Gnome Has Gone Too Far!

(rhythm: first part of *Old MacDonald Had A Farm*)

E

G	G	G	G	E	E	E
Nob -	by	Gnome	has	gone	too	far!

G	G	A	A	B
I	will	make	him	pay.

G	G	G	G	E	E	E
I	will	make	him	change	his	spell,

G	G	A	A	B
I	will	have	my	way!

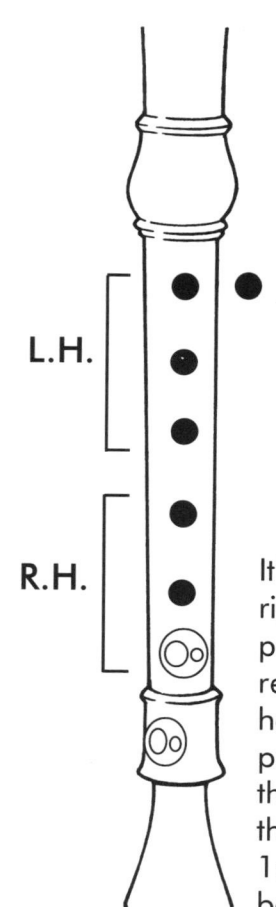

So the King set off up the great big hill, no-one waved, no-one moved, every statue stayed still.

insert sticker

It's now time to bring the right-hand into the correct position. Holding the recorder with the left-hand in its usual position, put the r.h. thumb behind the 4th hole to balance the recorder, and hold the 1st 3 fingers over the bottom 3 holes

Puff, Puff, Puff!

(rhythm: *Jingle Bells*)

E	G	E		E	G	E
Puff,	puff,	puff!		Pant,	pant,	pant!

C	C	C	C	B
Puff,	puff,	pant,	pant,	puff!

E	G	E	E	E	G	E
Cute	King	Dodge	was	hop	- ing	mad

B	B	B	B	B	B	E
And he'd	real	- ly		had	e	- nough.

The King ranted and raved and yelled and stamped his feet, but Nobby Gnome just laughed. "I'm not going to change the spell until you change your ways!" he told the King firmly. So in the end the King snapped, "All right! What must I do?"

insert sticker

Nobby Gnome Tells Cute King Dodge What He's Got To Do

(rhythm: *Humpty Dumpty Sat On A Wall*)

G	**G**	**E**	**E**	**G**	**G**	**E**
You	must	speak	to	Deid - re	and	Dave,

B	**B**	**G**	**G**	**B**	**B**	**B**	**G**
You	must	go	right	down	to	their	cave.

D	**D**	**D**	**B**	**B**	**B**	**D**	**D**	**D**	**B**
Tell	them	that	cave	peo -	ple	real -	ly	are	grand!

D	**D**	**D**	**C**	**C**	**C**	**B**	**B**	**A**	**G**
Say	that	their	carv -	ings	are	best	in	the	land!

y Gnome Heard Every Word!

(…ythm: *Oh Dear, What Can The Matter Be?*)

D		D C B B C D
Oh	dear,	what can the mat - ter be?

E	C	C B A A B C
Oh	dear,	what can the mat - ter be?

E	B	B A G G A B
Oh	dear,	what can the mat - ter be?

G G G G G G E
Nob - by Gnome heard ev - 'ry word!

And half way down the hill, the King found that he couldn't walk another step because he, too, had been turned to stone. But he could still see and he could still hear. Imagine how he felt when he spotted the cave people coming up the hill. Now they could get their own back. The King closed his eyes so that the cave people wouldn't see how embarrassed and ashamed he was.

insert sticker

The Kind Cave People Want To Help The King

(rhythm: first part of *Away In A Manger*)

low D

G	D	D	D D	G	G
They	trudged	up	to the	sta	- tue

G G	E	E	E	G
And he	op -	ened	one	eye,

G G	A	G	A	B
"We will	help	you"	they	said,

A	G G	A	G	A	B
"Now,	don't be	sad,	please	don't	cry".

Tears were dripping down the King's face because he felt so ashamed of himself. He'd treated the cave people so cruelly and yet they were still being kind to him.

insert sticker

From now on, all low Ds will have a line underneath them and all high Ds will have a line above them:
Low D̲ High D̄

L.H.
R.H.

He Wished That He Could Say Sorry

(rhythm: *For He's A Jolly Good Fellow*)

D̄	B	B	B	B	B	C		B	
He	wished	that	he	could	say	sor	-	ry,	

B	G	G	G	G	G	A		G	
He	wished	that	he	could	say	sor	-	ry,	

G	D̲	D̲	D̲	D̲	D̲	E		D̲	
He	wished	that	he	could	say	sor	-	ry,	

D̲	D̲		D̲	D̲		D̲	G	
If	on	-	ly	he		could	speak.	

But the statue king couldn't speak so he just stood still and silent while the cave people went further up the hill to talk to Nobby Gnome.

insert sticker

And This Is What They Said To The Gnome
(tune: *Hot Cross Buns*)

D̄ D Ḡ   D̄ D G
Nob - by Gnome,   Nob - by Gnome,

D̄ C B A G A B C D̄ D G
Make the King come back to life please, Nob - by Gnome,

B B B B B A G A B C A
He is ve - ry sor - ry, He is ve - ry sad,

D̄ C B A G A B C D̄ D G
If you'd make the King come back we'd all be glad.

So Nobby agreed to break the spell on the King, and the moment the spell was broken, everyone in Dodgem Land turned back into themselves again. But nobody except the King had any idea that time had stood still for a little while. The King went straight down to the cave.

insert sticker

And This Is What The King Said To The Cave People

(rhythm: *Morning Has Broken*)

D E D G   **B**
I've been so sil - ly,

D E D A   **C**
I can't be-lieve it,

D E D B   **D̄**
Wear-ing a hat, how

C B A B
sil - ly I've been.

D E D G   **B**
Thanks to your carv - ing

D E D A   **C**
I'll wear a crown now,

D E D B   **D̄**
If I am luck - y

C B A G
I'll find a queen!

So from that moment on the King always wore a crown instead of his chef's hat. And one day he was lucky because a beautiful young lady called Geraldine fell in love with him at first sight.

insert sticker

King Dodge And Queen Geraldine

(rhythm: *Lavender's Blue, Dilly Dilly*)

D̄	D̄	D̄	D̄	C	B	A	G	A	A	A	D̄
King	Dodge	said	"Please	will	you	mar-	ry	me,	Ger-	al-	dine?"

C	C	C	C	B	A	G	E	D	D	D	G
Ger-	ald-	dine	said	"If	I	mar-	ry	you	I'll	be	Queen!"

And so they got married. Nobby Gnome took the wedding service. Dave was the best man and Deidre the chief bridesmaid. And everyone in the whole of Dodgem Land was invited to a royal dodgem party after the wedding.

insert sticker

The Royal Dodgem Party

(tune: *She'll Be Coming Round The Mountain*)

D D   G G G G G   E D   E   G
They were dodg-ing round the moun-tains all day long.

G A   B B B B   D̄ D̄ D̄   B   A
They were dodg-ing round the moun-tains all day long.

D̄ C   B B B B A   G   **G G G G C   C**
They were dodg-ing round the moun-tains,   dodg-ing round the moun-tains,

B B B B   A A A   G
Dodg-ing round the moun-tains all day long.

And people from other kingdoms near and far came to look at the magnificent carvings of King Dodge, Queen Geraldine and many other scenes, so the cave people became very famous indeed.

insert sticker

And This Is What One Of The People Was Heard To Say . . .

(tune: *There's A Hole In My Bucket*)

F♯ (sharp)

G	A	B	D	D	E	G
I	just	love	all	these	carv	- ings,

D	E	G	D	E	G
They're	clev	- er,	they're	fun	- ny,

G	A	B	D	D	E	G
But	this	king	in	a	chef's	hat,

D	E	G	F♯	G
Well	that	is	so	cool!

And Queen Geraldine hugged her husband and said, "I don't mind whether you wear a chef's hat, a crown or a pair of flip-flops on your head. To me you're just Cute King Dodge!"

insert sticker

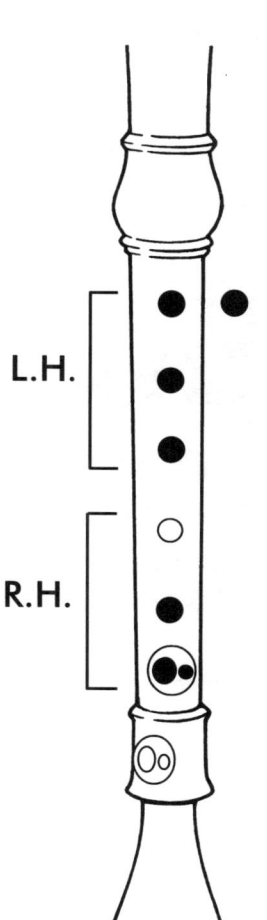

L.H.

R.H.

If you've enjoyed learning the recorder with Ann Bryant's Play Straight Away, why not think about starting to play the piano?

by Ann Bryant

The new adventure for young children and teachers of piano

A truly innovative and unique concept set in an exciting musical land of appealing characters and places which encourage and stimulate pupils to explore their creative imagination.

Pupil's Book One
ref: 3582A

Pupil's Book Two
ref: 3583A

Pupil's Book Three
ref: 3584A

Teacher's & Parent's Guide
ref: 5847A

Old MacPherson's Waterworld
ref: 5469A

Fantasmo Farmyard
ref: 5470A

The Wild Woods
ref: 5471A

Discover a whole new world in Keyland, join the Keyclub, meet new Keypals, receive special Keyclub gifts and get more stickers to stick!